Business

Ethics & its

Legal Aspects

For Ethics and Compliance

Professionals in Nigeria

Nicholas Aitalegbe

Published by

P E A C H E S

P U B L I C A T I O N S

Published in London, England by Peaches Publications, 2018.

www.peachespublications.com

British Library Cataloguing in Publication Data: A catalogue record for this book is available from the British Library.

ISBN: 978-0-244-41643-0

Book cover design: Peaches Publications
Typesetter: Winsome Duncan.

Contents

Dedication

To my good friends and support group – Biyi Pariola and Kunle Odesanya, who have both been keen about my work and writing. And to my loving and supportive wife, Nnennaya Annabel, who continue to be my chief critic for this work and others, in such a loving way that I simply enjoy and cherish.

And to my CRID family, clients and friends; for their steadfastness and support. Without them, this work would have been impossible to complete.

Acknowledgements

This work would not have been possible without the support of the team at CRID Corporate Compliance Services, especially my fellow directors, Jacob Kayode Olaleye and Paul Clark. I am especially indebted to my former school mates in OAU Ife, who have been supportive of my career goals and worked actively to provide me with strength to pursue these goals.

I am grateful to all those with whom I have had the pleasure to work with during this and other projects, especially at the University of Hertfordshire, Hatfield in the UK, for the numerous parts they have played.

Foreword

People often automatically assume that businesses are unethical. Business seems to be constantly linked to scandals. Given the media attention to bad ethical decisions, companies that practice good business ethics can distinguish themselves in the minds of their customers and their employees. The company culture helps determine the ethics of the organization. It is crucial that businesses behave ethically in every working relationship. The Nigerian terrain is fast changing to becoming a business environment of choice in the coming years. The impact played by both Houses of the National Assembly in the country cannot be over emphasized.

Introduction

A company's ethics will determine its reputation. Good business ethics are essential for the long-term success of an organization. Implementing an ethical programme will foster a successful company culture and increase profitability. Developing a business ethics programme takes time and effort, but doing so will do more than improve business, it will change lives.

A company's ethics will have an influence on all levels of business. It will influence all who interact with the company including customers, employees, suppliers, competitors, etc. All these groups will influence the way a company's ethics are developed. It is a two-way street, the influence goes both ways, which makes understanding ethics a very important part of doing business today. Ethics is very important, as news can now spread faster and farther than ever before.

Reasons for Writing the Book
Research has consistently demonstrated that when clear goals are associated with learning,

it occurs more easily and rapidly. With that in mind, let's review our goals for today.

At the end of this book, the readers should be able to:

- Define and understand ethics.
- Understand the benefits of ethics.
- Create strategies to implement ethics at work.
- Recognize social and business responsibility.
- Identify ethical and unethical behaviours.
- Learn how to make ethical decisions and lead with integrity.

1. What is Ethics?

A human being's personal ethics determine individual standards of right and wrong. Ethics allow people to determine what they should do in a given situation. Each person develops ethical standards, and it is the responsibility of everyone to examine personal morals and behaviour. In business, ethics refers to the behaviour relating to the moral problems that occur in business organizations.

What is Business Ethics?
People often automatically assume that businesses are unethical. Business seems to be constantly linked to scandals. Given the media attention to bad ethical decisions, companies that practice good business ethics can distinguish themselves in the minds of their customers and their employees. The company culture helps determine the ethics of the organization. It is crucial that businesses behave ethically in every working relationship.

Ethical Obligations:
• Employees: Companies need to treat all their employees ethically. Begin by providing employees with the rights guaranteed to them by the Ministry of Labour. Ethical businesses,

however, may go beyond the minimum requirements in the way that they treat their employees.
• Shareholders and investors: There is a moral obligation to pay back investors and meet the needs of shareholders, particularly low-level shareholders.
• Customers: Every business needs to build ethical customer relationships by providing safe products and honouring warranties. Consumers are growing more aware of which companies treat them fairly, and they will support the ones they trust.
• Community: Businesses have an ethical obligation to be involved in their local communities. This includes communities where they interact with customers and beyond.
• Vendors and Other Companies: Always deal ethically with vendors and other organizations you work with.

10 Benefits of Managing Ethics
Operating an ethical business has several rewards. The circumstances of each company will determine the results of managing ethics. There are, however, 10 common benefits that all companies have when they manage their business ethics.
Benefits:

- Ethical companies comply with all legal requirements and are less likely to be fined or sued.
- Consumers are more likely to support a business with a reputation as an ethical organization.
- Companies with ethical values improve their communities.
- Ethical rules save organizations from accidently violating the rights of employees or consumers.
- Employees' personal moral standards will improve at an ethical business.
- A fair working environment facilitates teamwork and productivity.
- Many successful financial business practices are reinforced by ethical business practices.
- Established ethical guidelines will lead a company in times of change and stress.
- Ethical companies retain employees and save money in turnover.
- There is personal satisfaction in doing the right thing.

Case Study
Jim Johnson owned a large investing brokerage in a large city. His firm had many clients who trusted them with their money, as they were known as an ethical and upstanding

business. When Jim retired a new CEO, Andrew, filled his place. Andrew brought in new managers who encouraged their employees to "borrow" from client's accounts. When it was discovered what the brokerage were doing, a nation-wide scandal erupted. Almost every customer closed their account with Andrew's brokerage and no new clients came to them due to their new unethical reputation. The brokerage never recovered, and soon after had to shut down.

Review Questions

1. Companies need to treat all their employees ethically?
a) True
b) False

2. Which is a benefit of running an ethical business?
a) Less likely to be fined or sued
b) Improve their community
c) More productivity
d) All of the above

3. What unethical behaviour caused the E.F. Hutton company to fail?
a) Charity donations
b) Cheque kiting
c) Reporting accounting errors
d) Paying fair wages

2. Implementing Ethics in the Workplace

Implementing ethics in the workplace is a complex but rewarding task. Every individual has a unique set of ethical standards. Allowing each person to follow his or her moral compass will result in varied results. Companies need to focus on implementing uniform ethical standards and rules throughout their organizations. Employees should never have to question whether they are doing the right thing.

Benefits
We discussed the top 10 benefits of managing ethics in the previous module. Implementing ethics in the workplace will also lead to better profits and long-term growth. Unethical business practices can cause immediate financial gain, but they will cost companies customers and employees over time. When unethical practices become public knowledge, it is difficult for a business to recover its reputation. Organizations with reputations for being ethical will also find it easier to earn credit, find investors, and expand into international markets. There are also benefits at the organizational level.

Organizational Benefits:
• Convinces employees that the company truly values ethical decision-making.
• Builds awareness of ethical issues.
• Creates an ethical guideline for employees to follow.

Guidelines for Managing Ethics in the Workplace

Managing ethics in the workplace requires certain tools. Every organization needs a Code of Ethics, a Code of Conduct, and Policies and Procedures, which we will discuss later. These tools direct the organization as leaders attempt to manage ethics.

Guidelines for Implementing and Managing Ethics:
• Give it time: Managing ethics is a process-oriented activity that requires time and constant assessment.
• Focus on behaviour: Do not give vague requirements; make sure that ethics management has an impact on behaviour.
• Avoid problems: Create clear codes and policies that will prevent ethical problems.
• Be open: Involve different groups in ethics programme and make decisions public.
• Integrate ethics: Make sure that all management programmes have ethical values.

- Allow for mistakes: Teach employees how to behave ethically, and do not give up when mistakes happen.

Roles and Responsibilities

The roles and responsibilities necessary to effectively implement workplace ethics will vary with each organization. A manager should be in place to oversee the ethics programme, but he or she will need the support provided by other positions. Smaller organizations may not need to fill all the roles listed below; determine what your company needs before executing an ethics programme.
Roles:

- CEO: The CEO of every company needs to support business ethics and lead by example.
- Ethics committee: An ethics committee will develop and supervise the programme.
- Ethics management team: Senior managers implement the programme and train employees.
- Ethics executive: An ethics executive or officer is trained to resolve ethical problems.
- Ombudsperson: This position requires interpreting and integrating values throughout the organization.

Case Study

Matt was a manager at a law firm, and felt that his employees, while not acting unethically, could use some guidance to be even more ethical. After clearing it with his boss, he started implementing a universal ethical standard for all employees at the firm. After some time, Matt had to sit down and discuss an unethical choice one of his employees, Paul, made. He let Paul explain himself before forming a solution. The mistake he made was minor, and the system was still new, so Matt decided to let it go with a warning. After thinking about the situation, he decided to appoint an ombudsman that could screen minor issues for him.

Review Questions

1. Which is not an organizational benefit of ethical companies?
a) Convinces employees that the company truly values ethical decision-making
b) Builds awareness of ethical issues.
c) Creates an ethical guideline for employees to follow
d) Less profits

2. Which is not a tool for managing ethics in the workplace?
a) Give it time
b) Immediately fire those who make ethical mistakes
c) Be open
d) Integrate ethics

3. Do all companies need to fill the roles of CEO, ethics committee, ethics management team, ethics executive, and ombudsman?
a) Yes
b) No

3. Employer/Employee Rights

An ethical organization can balance the rights of employees with the rights of the employer. The personal rights of each party may seem to conflict at times, and the privacy laws vary between states. Therefore, privacy policies are so important. Instituting clear privacy policies will prevent any confusion between employees and employers. When creating policies, employers need to remember that they are obligated to provide employees with a safe work environment that is free from harassment, and this may require what some people consider an invasion of privacy.

Privacy Policies

Employee privacy is a tangled legal issue. Companies collect detailed personal information about their employees for background checks and other reasons, and they need to clearly state the purpose of collecting this information and how it will be used in their privacy policy. Personal information must be protected and kept confidential, and the employees need to agree to the background checks.

Surveillance, drug testing, and searches are points of contention for many employees, and they need to be addressed in privacy policies. Employees argue that they have the right to personal privacy at work, but there are limits to their privacy as more businesses take drastic measures to prevent theft and harassment.

Surveillance: Organizations routinely monitor the phone and Internet usage of their employees while they are at work. Legally, these steps are protected in many countries because the company phones and Internet are company property. Security cameras are also used to ensure the safety of employees. Experts advise employers to include in their privacy policies, a warning to employees that they will be monitored. There are limits to the use of cameras. For example, cameras are not allowed in locker rooms or bathrooms. Always check the legal ramifications of using surveillance.

Drug Testing: Taking a drug test before beginning a new job is common, and employers also have the right to demand drug tests in the event of an accident or suspicion of drug use. Random drug tests, however, can be contested if they violate employee privacy. The policy on random drug testing need to be reasonable and clearly spelled out.

Companies are responsible for keeping drug test results private.

Searches: Privacy policies need to remind employees that their workspace and tools are company property, and that they are not responsible for any lost or damaged personal property. This should prevent any invasion of privacy claims if an employer who suspects theft searches a locker. Searches should be conducted carefully and with the instruction of senior management.

Harassment Issues
Companies are legally bound to provide a safe working environment for all their employees. Employees can sue their employers for not protecting them from harassment. The EEOC protects the rights of individuals from discrimination and harassment, regardless of ethnicity, sex, religion, sexual orientation, disability, age, etc. An employee who feels threatened or uncomfortable by any statement, gesture, or action may be experiencing harassment. An anti-harassment policy and training in harassment will help prevent harassment and protect the organization. Any harassment in the workplace needs to be confronted

immediately and the rights of the harassed employee protected.

Technology

As technology changes, so does the clarity about employer and employee rights. Employers have the right to expect their employees to work productively and represent the company well. On the other hand, employees have the right to personal privacy. Advances in technology provide employers with more ways to monitor employees. Social networking further complicates this issue.

Employees often post things online for their friends to see, but employers may be monitoring these posts well. It is becoming more common for people to lose their jobs because of posts on their social networking sites. A recent survey revealed that about half of employees feel that their social networks are not any business of their employers, but 60 percent of executives think that they have the right to monitor their representatives' social network behaviour. This use of social networks should be included in privacy policies to protect both employee and employer, but many companies cite personal conduct policies to validate their actions.

Case Study

Charlie, a PR manager, was drafting a new privacy policy for his company. New regulations forced the company to collect additional private information from their employees for various employment records. Charlie knew that a company's privacy policy had to explicitly state what the information they collected would be used for.

The company was also installing several new cameras around the building, so Charlie had to include that the surveillance system would be active and recording in non-private areas to ensure employee and company safety. He made sure to clarify the use of the surveillance tapes, stating that while the tapes would be retained, they would be secured and only be reviewed in the case of a crime being recorded.

Review Questions

1. Does personal information need to be protected and kept confidential for a company to be ethical?
a) Yes
b) No

2. Ethical companies protect the rights of individuals from discrimination and harassment, regardless of what?
a) Ethnicity
b) Age
c) Religion
d) All of the above

3. The use of social networks should be included in what, to protect both employee and employer?
a) Privacy policies
b) Employer agreement
c) Validation report
d) Test agreement

4. Business & Social Responsibilities

Most successful businesses operate with socially responsible business practices. Being socially responsible requires companies to integrate the needs of their stakeholders into the values and operations of their organizations. Stakeholders typically include investors, customers, employees, the community and the environment. Social responsibility strives to consider all these needs in their business practices.

Identifying Types of Responsibilities
There are different types of responsibilities related to businesses. Ethical organizations need to cover different areas of responsibility and consider the social ramifications of their actions.

Types:
• Legal: Socially responsible companies are obligated to meet legal requirements that govern their industries. Health and safety standards and fair treatment of employees fall under this type of responsibility.
• Financial: Financial responsibility is more than turning a profit. Financial ethics cover

everything from fair salaries to fair payments for raw materials and services as well as not price gouging customers.
• Philanthropic: Many organizations are being recognized for their philanthropy. Philanthropy can come from donations, service, education, and environmental programmes. Some companies consider the environment its own type of social responsibility.

Case Study 1

Jeff Swartz, CEO of Timberland, volunteered with an urban outreach in 1989 and donated 50 pairs of boots. This experience led to the beginning of a programme called the Path to Service that officially began in 1992. This programme helps employees become involved in different community projects. Over 95 percent of employees take advantage of the programme. The Path to Service attracted many employees who believed it to be a crucial benefit. GREEN (Grassroots, Reduce-reuse-recycle, Engagement, Education, and Neutral) followed in 2008, which focuses on building community gardens and playgrounds. The company also donates money and product for charitable purposes.

Handling Conflicting Social and Business Responsibilities

Sometimes social and business responsibilities conflict with each other. This is particularly true when social business practices cut into shareholder earnings. This is a struggle for most public corporations. Businesses need to provide their shareholders with earning to convince them to continue to invest their money into the company. Sometimes this means scaling back a social programme or waiting to implement one. Lean earnings and a poor economy complicate the balance between social responsibility and company growth. Without shareholders, however, the company will lose the wealth that backs social programmes and the community will face further losses.

Case Study 2

Jeff, a CEO of a graphic tee-shirt company, volunteered with an urban outreach programme and donated 50 shirts. He noticed that afterwards, his sales had gone up. He started a programme for his employees to become involved in community projects. Many employees participated in some way and paved the way for Jeff's company to grow an ethical and generous reputation.

This programme attracted future employees, who believed that the programme was a crucial benefit to working with Jeff. Eventually, Jeff's programme branched out to building or donating to community gardens and playgrounds. Because of these programmes, People were proud to work for him, and happy to buy his products. Soon, Jeff's Shirts was a household name in his region.

Review Questions

1. Which is not an area of responsibility that must be considered regarding social ramifications of their actions?
a) Legal
b) Financial
c) Philanthropic
d) Internal politics

2. What percentage of Timberland employees are involved in the Path to Service programme, which helps employees be involved in community programmes?
a) 1%
b) 10%
c) 25%
d) 95%

3. What typically conflicts with social responsibility?
a) Social earnings
b) Public needs
c) Business earnings
d) Summary decisions

5. Ethical Decisions

We should always attempt to make ethical decisions. It is possible, however, for two ethical people to make different decisions in a situation. In business, it is important that people understand ethical dilemmas and the ethical decision-making process.

The Basics
People typically use five different ethical standards to interpret the world around them. For the best results, put the different approaches together and choose the answers that best fit.

Ethical Standards
• Utilitarian approach: This approach focuses on the consequences of actions. The goal is to do more good than harm in a situation.
• Rights approach: Focusing on the rights of all involved defines this approach. It makes respecting the rights of others a moral obligation.
• Fairness approach: Fairness expects people to be treated equally. A based standard is used to determine actions that are unequal such as pay rate.
• Common Good approach: The conditions that affect all people are considered in the

common good approach. Systems and laws are created to ensure the welfare of everyone.
• Virtue approach: This approach uses virtues such as honesty, compassion, love, patience, and courage to guide behaviour.

Balancing Personal and Organizational Ethics

It is important to be ethical on a personal and organizational level. Personal ethics influence decision both inside and outside of work. These are based on personal beliefs and values. Organizational ethics determine workplace decisions. Managers and employees both face organizational ethics, and the company should have ethical standards in place.

Organizational ethics flow from the top down. Those in leadership need to promote ethical decisions by their example. Occasionally, personal and professional ethics will collide. In the event of an ethical dilemma, it is important to choose based on what is most important and what will do the most good for the parties involved.

Common Dilemmas

There are many different ethical dilemmas in business that are specific to industries. There are, however, common dilemmas that every organization will face.

- Honest accounting practices
- Responsibility for mistakes such as accidents, spills, and faulty product
- Advertising that is honest and not misleading
- Collusion with competitors
- Labour issues
- Bribes and corporate espionage

Law governs many of these dilemmas, but an ethical organization will make the right decision regardless of legal issues. Because these issues are so common, it is important to create ethical standards and train employees to behave accordingly.

Making Ethical Decisions

Before making any final decisions, use the following steps to make sure that you are making ethical decisions.

- Determine the ethics of a situation: Does the decision affect a group or have legal ramifications?
- Gather Information: Learn as much as possible about the situation and get the point of view from all parties involved.

- Evaluate Actions: Make different decisions based on the different ethical standards.
- Test Decisions: Would you be proud of this decision if it were advertised?
- Implement: Implement the decision and evaluate the results.

Overcoming Obstacles

There will always be temptation to act unethically. These obstacles are particularly difficult to overcome when other people are encouraging you to behave unethically. They may be in positions of authority or simply intimidating, but you do not have to give into them.

Overcome Obstacles:
- Sympathize: Do not attack unethical people. Sympathize with their situation but refuse to compromise your standards.
- Make them responsible: Do not quibble. Directly ask people if they want you to do something illegal or unethical. This removes their plausible deniability.
- Reason: Provide them with logical reasons for your refusal to compromise your integrity.
- Stay firm: Decide and stick to it. Do not let people wear you down.

• Take precautions: Keep a paper trail of your encounters and be prepared to defend yourself.

Case Study

Dave had to make an ethical decision and wasn't sure how to go about finding the best result. After doing some research, he decided to work out the end results of five different processes. He chose to compare the theoretical results of the Utilitarian, Rights Based, Fairness, Common Good, and Virtue approaches.

Dave considered several things in his process. What were the ramifications of his decision? Did he know everything he could about the situation? Would he be okay with if his choice was advertised? After he made sure to consider everything he could think of, he found his decision easy to make. In the end, what he chose benefitted his company and their reputation.

Review Questions

1. Typically, there are how many ethical standards for interpreting the world?
a) 3
b) 5
c) 8
d) 10

2. Organizational ethics flow from where?
a) Bottom up
b) Top down
c) Public domain
d) Employee actions

3. Honest accounting practices, accurate advertising, and taking responsibility for mistakes are examples of what?
a) Common dilemmas
b) Ethical targets
c) Laws
d) Rights of business

4. What is the first step to making ethical decisions?
a) Can the problem be ignored?
b) Does the decision have legal ramifications?
c) Can the issue be solved with more money?
d) Is there a way to make money from the situation?

5. Which is not a tool to be used when others are encouraging you to be unethical?
a) Bribery
b) Sympathy
c) Reason
d) Staying firm

6. Whistle Blowing

Whistle blowing is either seen as a public service or a petty act of tattle telling. Whistle blowers create public concern over misconduct. Blowing the whistle is not an easy decision to make. While legally protected, whistle-blowers take on serious personal risks by informing on their employers. There are circumstances, however, that need to be reported to protect the public.

Criteria and Risk
The term "whistle-blower" is British, and it comes from the whistles that the police used to carry to alert the public and other police to a crime. Whistle blowers point out serious infractions that break the law; risk public or employee health; fraud; or signs of corruption. Telling on a co-worker who was late is not whistle blowing.

Legal protection has been provided to whistle-blowers since the 1960s, and the laws have changed to keep up with the times. While there is legal protection for whistle-blowers, they do face retaliation. They may be fired for unrelated reasons, harassed, or intimidated. They may find it difficult to find another job because of their reputations as whistle-blowers.

The Process

There are two types of whistle-blowers: internal whistle-blowers and external whistle-blowers. Internal whistle-blowers go to someone within the organization to report a problem. Many companies have ways of doing this anonymously so that the employee will be protected from retaliation. External whistle-blowers go outside the organization with the issue. They go to law enforcement or the media. External whistle blowing is the best method for businesses that are corrupt from the top down. Once the whistle is blown, whistle-blowers need to protect their rights and possibly seek legal counsel to shield themselves from retaliation.

When You Should "Blow the Whistle"

Think carefully before blowing the whistle. Doing so is neither fun nor easy. There are situations, however, when blowing the whistle is the right thing to do. If the rights, health, or safety of others is knowingly compromised and no one will fix the problem, the whistle needs to be blown. It is the ethical thing to do.

Blowing the whistle legally requires you to have a "reasonable belief" that the violations occurred with company knowledge. This means that others could assume the same breaches occurred as the whistle-blower. It is best to have evidence of the misconduct before moving forward.

Case Study

Caroline worked at a large investment firm with thousands of clients. Caroline was a hard-working employee, and eventually was promoted to management. On her first day, the other managers sat down with her and explained that they would take a little bit of money from each account, because they felt their wages weren't high enough, but their boss wouldn't raise their pay.

Caroline went to her boss about this breach of ethics, but he secretly knew about it and participated. Seeing that she needed to report this externally, she got legal counsel to help her report this through the proper channels. Through her lawyer, Caroline also learned that she had legal protection as a whistle-blower.

Review Questions

1. whistle-blowers are protected under the law?
a) True
b) False

2. What are the two types of whistle-blowers?
a) Legal and Illegal
b) Social and Political
c) Red and Green
d) Internal and External

3. Blowing the whistle legally requires you to have _____ _____ that the violations occurred with company knowledge?
a) Reasonable belief
b) Unknown knowledge
c) Plausible deniability
d) Monetary motivation

7. Managerial Ethics

Managers have a responsibility to behave ethically and manage ethically. They set the example for all employees and will determine how effective ethics management can be. Ethical management provides several benefits, both to the company culture and financial gain of the organization.

Ethical Management
Ethical management balances the different responsibilities of modern business organizations.

Responsibilities:
• Profit: All companies are responsible to make a profit to survive and fulfil their other obligations.
• People: This includes employees, customers, shareholders, and the community.
• Planet: Sustainability and the preservation of resources is a growing responsibility for businesses.
• Principles: The ethics that govern the organization will help the company to act ethically in every area.

Identifying the Characteristics

There are many different characteristics of ethical management. There are three traits, however, that people identify with ethical management:

• Integrity: The manager behaves with integrity and leads by example.

• Transparency: The company and its managers are transparent and do not hide their actions.

• Utilitarianism: The organization and manager consider the happiness of the people involved in the organization.

Ensuring Ethical Behaviour

Because ethics and values are extremely personal, it is difficult to ensure that all employees will practice ethical behaviour. There are ways to promote ethical behaviour, however, by simply instilling a few basic rules.

• Develop an ethics management programme.

• Develop a code of ethics.

• Develop a code of conduct.

• Create policies and procedures that reflect the company ethics.

It is not enough to simply create codes, programmes, policies, and procedures. All rules must be enforced to be effective and curb unethical behaviour.

Case Study

Joseph was recently hired for an open position as a manager at a call centre. He was assigned to shadow and learn from Shaun, who had been a manager there for several years. Shaun told Joseph the four pillars of ethical management; Profit, People, Planet, Principles.

He continued, explaining that the company has a responsibility to pay back it's investors and increase its stock price for shareholders, to treat their employees, customers, and community with respect, to be sustainable and green, and to stand by the organization's core principles always. Shaun told Joseph that if he remembers the four P's, and acted with integrity, he'd make an excellent manager and a great fit with the company.

Review Questions

1. Being an ethical manager, you are responsible for what?
a) Profit
b) People
c) Principles
d) All of the above

2. Which is not a trait that is associated with ethical management?
a) Integrity
b) Transparency
c) Greed
d) Utilitarianism

3. What are ways to help promote ethical behaviour?
a) Develop an ethics management programme
b) Develop a code of ethics
c) Create policies and procedures that reflect the company ethics
d) All of the above

8. Unethical Behaviour

Employees will act unethically from time to time. It is important to be able to identify unethical behaviour and address it. A successful manager should also be able to prevent poor behaviour and intervene before the behaviour escalates.

Recognize & Identify
Stress can take its toll on employees, who will occasionally act out at work. When unethical behaviour begins, managers need to identify it as soon as possible. Allowing unethical behaviour to continue will have long-term consequences for the company.

Typical Unethical Behaviour
• Abusing sick leave
• Lying to customers
• Cutting corners
• Covering up mistakes
The behaviour may seem minor; most people are guilty of at least one these incidents. These minor lapses in ethical judgment, however, can lead to more unethical behaviour later.

Preventing

Preventing unethical behaviour is much easier than dealing with the aftermath. We have already addressed ways to prevent unethical behaviour such as implementing a code of ethics and ethical policies and taking swift action. Another tactic that can prevent unethical behaviour is improving job satisfaction. Employees often react to situations they feel are unfair.

Addressing

Unethical behaviour needs to be addressed carefully. It is important to discuss the situation face-to-face. If the behaviour specifically violates company policy, remind the person about the policy. If the situation is a grey area, you may have to explain why it was not ethical. Approach the situation calmly and allow people to explain their actions. Do not jump to conclusions and understand that people sometimes need guidance making ethical decisions. Should unethical behaviour continue, take the necessary disciplinary action.

Interventions

Workplace interventions occur when people are concerned about the welfare of their co-workers. Interventions are usually used to help co-workers with addiction problems such as alcohol or drug abuse. They can also be held when assisting co-workers to deal with unethical behaviour specifically committed at work. There are certain steps that need to happen if anyone chooses to hold an intervention.

- Call an interventionist: A professional is needed to handle the situation.
- Create an action plan: Plan how the intervention should go.
- Meet: Have the group meet beforehand to iron out details.
- Intervention: Hold the intervention for an hour or two, and dialogue without judgment.
- Treatment: Help the co-worker find treatment if he or she decides it is necessary.

Case Study

Viola was notorious for cutting corners or blaming others for her mistakes. She would often make mistakes on her work due to her minimum effort put in, and she would pin the blame on one of her colleagues. Eventually, her manager got fed up with her behaviour and had a meeting with her.

Her manager reminded Viola that what she was doing was against company policy and showed disregard for the well-being of other's work and professional reputation. Viola didn't think she had done anything wrong, and resented being called out on her behaviour. Her manager explained exactly what she did wrong and how she could act more ethically, but she still refused to change. She quit soon after.

Review Questions

1. It is important to address minor unethical behaviour like cutting corners and abusing sick leave because it may lead to more unethical behaviour in the long term?
a) True
b) False

2. It is easier to deal with the aftermath of unethical behaviour than it is in preventing it?
a) True
b) False

3. What should be done before a workplace intervention is preformed?
a) Call an interventionist
b) Create an action plan
c) Meet beforehand
d) All of the above

9. Ethics in Business I

Ethics in business requires diligence and hard work. The entire organization needs to be on the same page for people to make ethical decisions. It is important to create codes and principles to guide people. The ethical principles and codes that the company uses, however, should directly reflect the needs of the business.

Organization Basics

When building an ethical business, it is important that the roles and responsibilities of each member of the company are clearly outlined. An organizational chart will help determine how an ethics programme will run. There will need to be a chain of command overseeing the ethics programme. The interrelationships of these roles should be established along with the ethical standards that must be embraced at every level. Remember that business ethics begin at the top of the organizational chart.

Addressing the Needs

The needs of the organization should be determined by surveying both customers and the employees. Most companies have a plan to gauge customer satisfaction. The company culture, however, is a clue to the ethics of the business. Anonymous surveys allow people to describe how the company runs and what it needs to increase ethical behaviour on every level of the workplace.

Needs to Address:

- Company values
- Personal responsibility
- Employee participation
- Conflicts
- Trust

Ethical Principles

An organization's ethical principles should reflect its needs. For example, a company that ranks low in personal responsibility probably has a bullying problem and needs to create principles that address the issue. There are a few basic business ethics principles that most companies can benefit from instituting.

• Trust: Customers and employees react better to a company they trust, and they feel trusts them.

• Clarity: Make sure that all documents, codes, principles, etc. are clear and easy to understand.

• Community: Support community involvement.

• Accurate records: Keep all records and accounting up-to-date and above suspicion.

- Respect: Treat all people with respect, regardless of their position.

Case Study

Kevin was the owner of an elective surgery practice. He knew that maintaining an ethical and responsible reputation was crucial in his field and acted on the belief that ethical behaviour started at the top and cascaded down. To ensure a high level of organizational integrity, he created a company code of ethics and appointed an office ombudsman to ensure it was being followed.

His ombudsman would address office issues, and reinforced company values, personal responsibility, and employee participation in discussions. Because of his work in creating an ethical and friendly environment, his employees felt fulfilled and happy in their positions and customers felt that his practice was trustworthy, with many repeat customers.

Review Questions

1. Business ethics begin where on the organizational chart?
a) Middle
b) Bottom
c) Employee level
d) Top

2. Who should be surveyed to determine the needs of an organization?
a) Employees
b) Employees and customers
c) Customers
d) Politicians

3. What should an organization's ethical principles reflect?
a) It's needs
b) Profit margin
c) Wages increases
d) Production ability

10. Ethics in Business II

A successful ethics programme needs safeguards and a clear code of ethics. To get the most from a programme, it is necessary to evaluate and adjust from time to time. Becoming an ethical business is a process that takes time, but it is possible to succeed if all those involved uphold the programme and continue working towards a common goal.

Ethical Safeguards
Ethical safeguards need to be in place to ensure ethical behaviour. Safeguards take away the excuse that employees do not know better. Safeguards do more than protect the company; they help bring in work. In fact, many government agencies demand that those they contract with have ethical safeguards in place.
Examples:
- Code of Conduct
- Employee training
- Ethics audits

Developing a Code of Ethics
A Code of Ethics is the foundation of an ethics programme. The Code of Ethics needs to address certain issues.

• Laws and regulations: All legal requirements need to be considered.
• Company needs: Consider the needs of the organization when creating a code.
• Ethical values: Use the ethics and values of the company. Include two examples for each value.
• Wording: Make sure that everyone knows that they must abide by the Code of Ethics.
Update the code each year, and make sure that everyone has a copy of these guidelines.

Performing an Internal Ethics Audit
An internal ethics audit utilizes several different sources. An auditor (or a committee, if there is no auditor) usually goes over the information to determine if any adjustments need to be made.
Sources:
• Surveys
• Interviews
• Documents
• Focus Groups
• Direct Observation
The audit is used to evaluate the design, execution, and effectiveness of the organization's ethical objectives, programmes, and activities.

Upholding the Ethics Programme

There needs to be complete buy-in for an ethics programme to be successful. It is not implemented to keep employees from stealing office supplies. Managers must uphold the ethics programme by adhering to it themselves and holding all their employees to the same standards. Managers are also responsible for ensuring that employees have all the necessary resources to be successful, and that they are fully trained in any new policies or procedures.

Case Study

Kevin, hoping to maintain or even increase integrity in his practice, started doing internal ethics audits. He sent a survey to all his employees to complete, which would cover how they felt about the practice's behaviour, reputation, and their personal feelings on their place at the company. He also conducted interviews with managers, asking for their suggestions on how to make sure their reputation is spotless and employee satisfaction is high.

With their suggestions, he opted to update their code of ethics every year to keep up with the changing needs of his employees and customers. On top of that, he started having monthly open ethics meetings, and established a board of ethics that employees could participate in.

Review Questions

1. Many government agencies demand that
_____ _____ are in place before they do
business with private companies?
a) Ethical safeguards
b) Profit safeguards
c) Labiality safeguards
d) Employee retentions

2. A Code of Ethics is the foundation of an
ethics programme. The Code of Ethics needs to
address what issues?
a) Laws and regulations
b) Company needs
c) Ethical values
d) All of the above

3. Who is exempt from the Code of Ethics?
a) CEO
b) Shareholders
c) No one
d) Board of directors

4. Why is it important to perform an internal
ethics audit?
a) Evaluate the design of the ethics programme
b) Evaluate the effectiveness of the ethics
programme
c) Evaluate the execution of the ethics
programme
d) All of the above

11. Nigerian National Ethics and Value Bill

Introduction

The Senate at its Plenary Sitting on Thursday, 1st March 2018, deliberated on the Agency for National Ethics and Values Compliance (Establishment, etc.) Bill, 2018 (HB. 519). After debates on its general principles, which was led by the Senate Leader, **Distinguished Senator Ahmad Lawal,** the Bill was read for the Second Time and referred to the Senate Committee on Information and National Orientation, for further legislative action, vide Senate Order of Referral, dated 6th March 2018 to report back with its recommendations. It should be stated for the avoidance of doubt that the Bill is a House of Representatives Bill. It was passed in the House on the Tuesday, 17th October 2017.

The Nigerian House of Representatives at its plenary on Thursday, 19th May 2016 read the National Agency for Ethics and Values Bill, 2016 (HB:519) the second time and referred same to the Committee on Information, National Orientation, Ethics and Values for further legislative action. At the public hearing, there were 13 memoranda with argument in favour of the Bill and 1 memorandum with argument against the Bill, from the National Orientation Agency, siting duplication of functions. The general consensus is that the Bill could not have come at a better time than now that Nigeria need to have a sustainable structure that will have a clear mandate to ensure compliance of Nigerians (including corporate Nigerians) with the provisions of Chapter 2:23 of the 1999 Constitution of the Federal Republic of Nigeria (as amended) which says: "The National Ethics shall be Discipline, integrity, Dignity of Labour, Social Justice, Religious Tolerance, Self-Reliance and Patriotism."

Methodology:
The Committee in carrying out this assignment used the following methods:
a) conducted a Public Hearing on the 6th and 7th of December 2016;
b) took oral and written submissions from stakeholders and general public;
c) had interactive sessions with various interest groups; and
d) met severally to consider the opinions gathered and had a clause by clause consideration of the Bill.

Recommendations and Actions:

The Committee finds it pertinent to remark that the purposes for which the Bill under consideration seeks to satisfy are commendable. Due to the amendments of certain sections, renumbering became necessary in retaining clauses. Some clauses were deleted and others reframed for clarity purposes. The details would be found in the next pages of this report.

Part I - Preliminary

1. There is established an Agency to be known as the Agency for National Ethics and Values Compliance (in this Act referred to as the "Agency") which shall have the functions and powers assigned to it by this Act.
2. The Agency:
a. shall be a body corporate with perpetual succession and a common seal;
b. may sue and be sued in its corporate name;
c. shall be organized as an independent Agency in the Presidency;
d. is charged with the responsibility to receive and process disclosure of impropriety made by anyone to the Office of the President.

3. The objectives of the Agency shall be to:

a. monitor and regulate the activities of establishments in both public and private sectors in order to maintain high standards of workplace ethics in Nigeria;
b. develop and enforce ethical standards to ensure that the actions and behaviours of citizens or residents of Nigeria conform to the highest standards of National Ethics as provided in Chapter II of the 1999 Constitution of the Federal Republic of Nigeria as amended.

4. The National Ethics shall be:
a. Discipline;
b. Integrity;
c. Dignity of Labour;
d. Social Justice;
e. Religious Tolerance;
f. Self-Reliance;
g. Patriotism.

5. The motto of the Federal Republic of Nigeria shall be:
a. Unity and Faith;
b. Peace and Progress.

6. In fulfilling its mandate, the Agency shall, in addition to the values and principles under this Act, observe and accommodate the following:

a. diversity of Nigerian people;
b. impartiality and gender equity; and,
c. the rules of natural justice.

7. It shall be the duty of every citizen to:
a. abide by the Constitution, respect its ideals and its institutions, the National Flag, the National Anthem, the National Pledge, and legitimate authorities;
b. help to enhance the power, prestige and good name of Nigeria, defend Nigeria and render such national service as may be required;
c. respect the dignity of other citizens and the rights and legitimate interests of others and live in unity and harmony and in the spirit of common brotherhood;
d. make positive and useful contributions to the advancement, progress and wellbeing of the community where he resides;
e. render assistance to appropriate and lawful agencies in the maintenance of law and order;
f. declare his income honestly to appropriate and lawful agencies and pay his tax promptly:

8. Every establishment in Nigeria shall develop programmes to combat unethical behaviours, and these shall include:

a. establishment of Ethics and Values Unit to ensure compliance under the provisions of this Act and workplace ethics;

b. designation of National Ethics \ Compliance Officer(s) at its management level; and

c. regular ethics training for its employees:

9. No persons shall practice the profession of Ethics Compliance in Nigeria unless the person is certified in accordance with this Act.

Part II - Administration

The Agency shall consist of:

a. the Office of the Director-General;

b. the Directorates of:

i. Finance and Administration;

ii. Training and Licensing;

iii. Investigation and Compliance;

iv. Surveillance & Intelligence;

v. Research & Planning; and

vi. State Offices Operation:

c. departments and units as may be required to assist the Director-General in the performance of the duties of the Agency under this Act:

11. The Agency shall have a Governing Board (in this Act referred to as the "Board") which shall comprise the following:

a. The Vice President of the Federal Republic of Nigeria as Chairman;
b. Secretary to the Government of the Federation
c. Attorney- General & Minister of Justice;
d. Minister of Industry, Investment & Trade;
e. Minister of Information and Culture;
f. Minister of Labour and Productivity;
g. Minister of Education;
h. Minister of Interior;
i. The Inspector-General of Police; and,
j. The Director-General of the Agency.

12. The Board shall appoint other persons of proven integrity and with considerable experience to serve as members of the Board to represent the interest of the:
a. Professional & Business communities;
b. Christian bodies;
c. Muslim bodies;
d. Traditional rulers; and,
e. Civil Society Organizations

13. The Board shall make standing orders regulating its proceedings.

14. The members of the Board, other than the Director-General, shall be part-time members of the Agency and at no time would the members exceed 20 persons.

15. The numbers of meetings in a year and the emoluments of the members of the Board will be in conformity with the rules governing remunerations of other Federal Government Agencies Board.

16. The functions of the Board shall be to:
a. direct the Agency in policy formulation;
b. give strategic direction to the Agency in the performance of its functions as stipulated in this Act;
c. establish and maintain strategic linkages and partnerships with other stakeholders in the rule of law and other governance sectors;
d. deal with reports, complain of abuse of power, impropriety and other forms of misconduct on the part of the Agency or its staff;
e. review and approve the financial statements of the Agency; and,
f. review and approve the annual estimates and budget of the Agency.

17 The functions of the Agency shall be to:
a. enforce citizens and residents of Nigeria to comply with the National Ethics as may be provided for in this Act;
b. regulate the standard of ethics in private and government establishments;

c. develop a set of professional and ethical standards to guide all public and private establishments to uphold National Ethics;

d. establish a National Ethics and Values Professional Certification Board;

e. conduct trainings and examinations for the award of various levels of certificate to person willing to practice as Ethics Compliance Officer;

f. facilitate the creation and supervise the "Ethics and Values Unit" in both public and private establishments;

g. monitor and evaluate the practices, procedures and code of ethics of private and public establishments operating in Nigeria (including professional bodies);

h. identify unethical practices of private and public establishments and secure the revision of the procedures;

i. research and identify all ethical issues that negatively impact on Nigeria development and make recommendations to the President;

j. issue Certificate of National Ethics Compliance to individual and establishments;

k. collaborate with anti-graft agencies as it relates to the control of unethical behaviours:

18. The Agency shall have its Investigation and Compliance Directorate headed by a senior police officer from the Nigeria Police

Force; and the directorate shall be charged with responsibility of monitoring, arresting and conducting investigation into any suspected breach of the National Ethics;

19. Any establishment or person that breach any provision of this Act or contravenes the provisions of sections 8 and 9 is guilty of an offence and is on conviction liable to a fine of N250,000 for each day the contravention continues.

20. Any violation of ethical standards shall lead to an offence of disciplinary nature and shall be prosecuted by the Agency for the purpose of the:
a. protection of the rights of citizens and residents of Nigeria or visitors to Nigeria;
b. freezing or confiscation of proceeds of the breach or related to the breach;
c. payment of compensation;
d. recovery or protection of public property; and
e. other punitive and disciplinary measures.

21. Any statement in any declaration that is found to be false by any authority or person authorized in that behalf to verify it, shall be deemed to be a breach of this Act.

22. If any person required to furnish information under this Act fails to do so or in purported compliance with such requirement to furnish information knowingly or recklessly makes any statement which is false shall be guilty of an offence and liable on conviction to a fine of N500,000 or imprisonment for a term of six months or both.

23. Any person who willfully obstructs, interferes with, assaults or resists any officer of the Agency in the execution of his duty under this Act or who aids, invites, induces or abets any other person to obstruct, interfere with, assault or resist any such officer of the Agency, shall be guilty of an offence and liable on conviction to a fine of N500,000 or imprisonment for a term of six months or both.

24. Where an offence under this Act, which has been committed by
a body corporate, is proved to have been committed with the connivance of or attributable to any neglect on the part of a director, manager or similar officer of the establishment, the body corporate shall be fined and he person prosecuted and sentenced or fined or both.

25. Where a body corporate is liable for breach and found culpable four consecutive times under this Act but found to be guilty one more time of any offence under this Act, the court may order that the body corporate shall thereupon be wound up and all its assets forfeited to the Federal Government of Nigeria.

26. Any person who in respect of any complaint lodged by him knowingly makes to the Agency any statement, whether or not in writing, which is false in any material particular, shall be guilty of an offence and shall on conviction be sentenced to imprisonment for one year without the option of a fine.

27. The Agency shall have all powers necessary or expedient for the efficient and effective execution of its functions under this Act or any other written law.

28. Without prejudice to the generality of section 27 of this Act, the Agency shall have power to:
a) to conduct investigation into any suspected breach of the National Ethics;

b) conduct mediation, conciliation and negotiation on conflicts that has arisen from neglect of the National Ethics;

c) monitor the ethical practices of both public and private establishments and order for the revision of their procedures where necessary;

d) institute & conduct proceedings in court for purposes of prosecution of breach of National Ethics or any section of this Act;

e) establish and maintain strategic partnerships with Non-Governmental Organizations and other stakeholders in the advancement of ethics, rule of law and good governance;

f) receive complaints on the breach of public trust and breach of the Code of Ethics by public officers or delay in prosecution by antigraft agencies;

g) investigate and recommend to the Director of Public Prosecutions the prosecution of any acts or breach or violation of public trust, Codes of Ethics or other matter prescribed under this Act or any other law;

h) impose fine for violation of National Ethics as entrenched in this Act or any ethics standard introduced by the Agency;

i) access buildings, relevant records, documents, personnel, electronic materials and computerized records generated, or in the possession of, any persons or organization for the purpose of investigations, financial reviews, forensic audits, evaluations or other activities related to suspected breach of National Ethics;

j) recommend appropriate action to be taken against public officers alleged to have engaged in unprofessional and unethical conduct;

k) oversee the enforcement of public trust and Codes of Ethics prescribed for public officers;

l) advise, on its own initiative, any person on any matter within its functions;

m) request and obtain professional advice from persons or organizations;

n) summon in writing any person who in the opinion of the Agency is in the position to testify on any matter before him, to give evidence in the matter and any person who fails to appear when required to do so shall be guilty of an offence under this Act;

o) carry out joint operations with the Nigeria Police Force and establish a special unit, under the Nigeria Police Force, charged with responsibility of monitoring and arresting violators of National Ethics;

p) establish and operate Ethics and Values Corps (EVACORPS) in collaboration with Non-Governmental Organizations, to compel citizens and residents of Nigeria, including corporate Nigerians to obey rules and ethics standards, using fines to correct disobedience.

q) open operation offices inside all the State and Local Government Secretariats across the country;

r) develop criteria and conduct examinations to determine competence in the practice of compliance and ethics profession through certification programmes for Certified National Ethics Professional (CNEP);

s) register professionals and training institutes to provide short courses for candidates who are preparing for the Certified National Ethics Professional (CNEP) Examinations;

t) charge and retain, to offset its overhead expenses, fees for services rendered to establishments, including fees for certification as National Ethics Professional;

u) accept and retain, for its operations, gifts, grants or donations from any person(s) or establishment(s) unless the conditions attached are inconsistent with the functions of the Agency;

v) borrow on such terms and conditions as the Board may approve, such sums of money as the Agency may require, in the exercise of the functions conferred on it by this Act;

w) remove and make copies of any documents for the purpose of investigating breach of National Ethics;

x) obtain from the Ethics Compliance Units of private and public establishments, not later than April 30 and October 31 of each year, semi-annual reports summarizing the activities of the Ethics Compliance Units during the immediately preceding six-month periods ending March 31 and September 30. Such reports shall include, but need not be limited to:

i. description of significant problems, abuses, and deficiencies relating to the administration of ethics control measures during the reporting period;

ii. description of the recommendations for corrective action made by the Ethics Compliance Unit during the reporting period;

iii. identification of each significant recommendation described in previous semi-annual reports on which corrective action has not been completed;

iv. summary of matters referred to prosecuting authorities and the prosecutions and convictions which have resulted.

29. In addition to the powers under this Act, the Agency shall ensure access to all parts of

the Federal Republic of Nigeria and shall have the power to:
a. acquire, hold, charge and dispose movable and immovable property; and
b. do or perform all such other things or acts for the proper discharge of its functions under this Act or any written law.

30. The Agency, in consistent with the core principles and critical components for the success of donors assisted programmes such as transparency, accountability and integrity, shall require all recipients of International Grants and Aids to:
a) adhere to the highest ethical standards in the conduct of donor-supported activities;
b) exercise the utmost care and integrity in the management, use and appropriation of grant funds and any assets procured with Donors' Resources;
c) exercise diligence in ensuring that Donors' Resources are used for their intended purposes and reach the intended beneficiaries;
d) register with the Agency any agreement or Code of Conduct ascribed to;
e) notify the Agency upon discovery of conduct which is inconsistent with the National Ethics:

31. The Agency shall:

a) investigate violations of any agreement or any Code of Conduct for Recipients of International Grants and Aids;

b) establish the principles and standards of conduct required of all recipients of International Grants and Aids.

c) establish standards for financial management systems and practices to properly record, reconcile and report on the use, receipt and status of Donors' Resources

d) ensure that Donors' Resources are not used to support, finance or promote violence, aid terrorists or fund unethical activities.

32. The Agency shall:

a) monitor the Recipients of International Grants and Aids to ensure they comply with the international donors' requirements;

b) provide compliance technical assistance to the grantees;

c) build the capacity of the grantees to enable them align their reports with international standards of Donor Agencies:

d) have power to charge and receive fees, from Recipients of International Grants and Aids, to offset its overhead expenses for providing compliance technical assistance.

33. Recipients of International Grants and Aids shall obtain from the Agency, Certificate of National Ethics Compliance to qualify to receive international grants.

34. There shall be National, State and Local Government Secretariats of the Agency. The Secretariats shall comprise of such:
a) professional, technical and administrative officers and support staff, as may be recruited or appointed by the Agency in the discharge of its functions under this Act;
b) civil servants as may be seconded by the Federal or State Civil Service Commission to the Agency upon its request;
c) Police officers may be posted by the Inspector-General of Police to the Agency upon its request:

35. The Agency may establish committees for the effective discharge of its functions.

36. The Agency may admit into the membership of committees established under section 35 other persons whose knowledge and skills are found necessary for the functions of the Agency.

37. Any person admitted into the Agency under section 36 may attend the meetings of

the Agency and participate in its deliberation, but shall have no power to vote.

38. The business and affairs of the Committees shall be conducted in accordance as constituted in its procedure.

39. The Agency shall:
a) through an open, transparent and competitive recruitment process appoint suitably qualified persons as staff to carry out the functions of the Agency;
b) in the appointment of employees, ensure that at least one-third of the employees are of either gender; and
c) ensure the appointments reflect ethic and regional diversity of the people of Nigeria.

40. The Agency shall be headed by a Director-General to be appointed by the President on the recommendation of the Chairman of the Board.

41. A person shall be qualified for appointment as the Director-General of the Agency if the person:
a) is a citizen of Nigeria;
b) possesses a professional certificate or postgraduate degree; and

c) has had at least fifteen years proven experience and demonstrated ability and a distinguished career in any of the following fields:
i. Ethics or Governance;
ii. Accounting or Audit;
iii. Public Administration;
iv. Leadership or Trusteeship;
v. Economics;
vi. Social Studies;
vii. Law;
viii. Religious Studies or Philosophy;
ix. Fraud Investigation;
x. Public Relations and Media;
xi. Defense and Security

42. A person shall not be qualified for appointment as Director-General if the person:
a) is a member of a governing body of a political party;
b) is an un-discharged bankrupt;
c) has been convicted of a felony; or breach of public trust
d) has been removed from public office for contravening the provisions of the Nigeria Constitution, this Act or any other law.

43. The Director-General shall take and subscribe to the oath of office.

44. The Director-General shall hold office for a term of four (4) years and shall be eligible for reappointment.

45. The Director-General shall be:
a. the Chief Executive Officer of the Agency;
b. the Accounting Officer of the Agency; and
c. responsible for:
i. carrying out the decisions of the Agency;
ii. supervision of other employees; and
iii. the day to day administration and management of the affairs of the Agency.

46. The Agency shall be divided into directorates to be headed by Executive Directors. A person shall be qualified for appointment, recruitment, secondment or promotion to any of the positions of the Executive Directors of the Agency if the person:
- holds an educational qualification not below a degree (or professional certificate of a degree equivalent) in any of the fields listed in section 41c (i-xi); and,
- has knowledge and experience of not less than fifteen years in the fields of study relevant to the position.

47. The Executive Directors shall be assisted by Heads of Departments and State Compliance Officers.

48. A person shall be qualified for appointment, recruitment, secondment (by the Civil Service Commission) or promotion to any of the positions of the Heads of Department or State Compliance Officers of the Agency if the person:
a) holds an educational qualification not below a degree (or professional certificate of a degree equivalent) from a recognized educational institution; and,
b) has had a distinguished career as well as knowledge and experience of not less than ten (10) years in any of the fields listed in section 41c (i-xi); or,
c) is a police officer of not less than the rank of Assistant Commissioner of Police, as may be posted by the Inspector-General of the Police to the Agency upon its request; or,
d) is an expert as may be hired with the approval of the Board, as contract staff to provide technical supports especially in the areas of forensic audit, grant management, arbitration and for other job schedules.

49. Contract Staff that shall be recruited in pursuant to section 48 (d) shall be appointed

in the first instance for a period of five years and shall be eligible for re-appointment, subject to good performance, for such further period as the Board may, from time to time, determine and on such terms as to emolument and otherwise as may be specified in his/her letter of appointment and as may, from time to time, be approved by the Board.

50. For the purposes of this Act, a police officer who is posted by the Inspector-General of Police or public officer who is seconded by the Civil Service Commission shall:
a) have the same benefits in the same manner as an employee recruited directly by the Agency under this Act; and,
b) be required to execute any instruction, orders and directions of the Agency.

51. Members and the employees of the Agency shall subscribe to the code of conduct as set out by the Agency in its manuals, sign a conflict of interest declaration form and be guided at all times by the standard operating procedures of the Agency.

52. The Agency shall identify ethical issues that can improve interpersonal and corporate relationships and produce documentary regular reports that shall engineer the

conscience of the citizenry to improve the ethical culture of the nation.

53. The Agency shall direct every Ministries, Departments and Agencies (MDAs) of the governments to establish Ethics and Values Unit within the MDAs to carry on the following duties:
a) provide coordination for control measures designed by the Agency to promote ethical cultured work place in MDAs;
b) receive and investigate complaints or information from employee of the MDAs concerning the possible existence of an activity constituting a violation of National Ethics;
c) carry out quarterly review and submit report to the Agency, with a copy to the head of the MDA, on ethical issues that may affect the economy, efficiency and effectiveness in the administration of their establishment or the nation;
d) provide a means for keeping the head of the MDA and the Agency fully and currently informed about problems and deficiencies relating to compliance with National Ethics and the necessity for and progress of corrective action.

54. There shall be a Certified National Ethics Professional of no lower rank than a deputy director who shall be the Ethic Compliance Director in all MDAs.

55. The Ethics Compliance Director shall report to and be under the general supervision of the head of the MDA involved or, to the extent such authority is delegated, the officer next in rank below such head, but shall not report to, or be subject to supervision by any other officer of such MDA.

56. Neither the head of the MDA nor the officer next in rank below such head shall prevent or prohibit the Ethics Compliance Director from initiating, carrying out, or completing any investigation.

57. The Agency shall direct every private establishments operating in Nigeria to establish Ethics and Values Unit within their establishment to carry on the following duties:
a) provide coordination for control measures designed by the Agency to promote ethical cultured work place in Nigeria.
b) receive and investigate complaints or information from employee or customer of the establishment concerning the possible

existence of an activity constituting a violation of National Ethics;

c) carry out quarterly review and submit report to the Agency, with a copy to the Chief Executive Officer of the establishment on ethical issues that may affect the economy, efficiency and effectiveness in the administration of their establishment or the nation;

d) provide a means for keeping the head of the establishment and the Agency fully and currently informed about problems and deficiencies relating to compliance with National Ethics and the necessity for and progress of corrective action.

58. The seal of the Agency shall be such device as may be determined by the Board and shall be kept by the Director-General.

59. The affixing of the seal shall be authenticated by the Director-General or any other person authorized in that behalf by a resolution of the Board.

60. Any document purporting to be under the seal of the Agency or issued on behalf of the Agency shall be received in evidence and shall be deemed to be so executed or issued, as the

case may be, without further proof, unless the contrary is proved.

61. Nothing done by a member of the Agency or by any person working under the instructions of the Agency shall, if done in good faith for the purpose of executing the powers, functions or duties of the Agency under this Act, render such member or officer personally liable for any action, claim or demand.

Part III - Financial Provisions

62. The funds of the Agency shall consist of:
(a) monies allocated by Appropriation Act of the National Assembly for the Agency;
(b) any grants, gifts, donations or other endowments given to the Agency;
(c) Such funds as may vest in or accrue to the Agency in the performance of its functions under this Act or under any other written law.

63. Any funds donated or lent to, or gift made to the Agency shall be disclosed and made public before use.

64. Staff and member of the Agency shall be paid such remuneration or allowances as the

Salaries and Remuneration Agency shall approve.

65. At least three months before the commencement of each financial year, the Agency shall cause to prepare estimates of the revenue and expenditure of the Agency for that year.

66. The annual estimates shall make provision for all the estimated expenditure of the Agency for the financial year concerned and in particular, shall provide for the:
(a) payment of remuneration in respect of the members and staff of the Agency;
(b) Payment of pensions, gratuities and other charges in respect of benefits which are payable out of the funds of the Agency;
(c) Maintenance of the buildings and grounds of the Agency;
(d) funding of training, research and development of activities of the Agency; and,
(e) creation of such funds to meet contingent liabilities in respect of benefits, insurance or replacement of buildings or installations, equipment and in respect of such other matters as the Agency may think fit.

67. The annual estimates shall be approved by the Board before the commencement of

the financial year to which they relate and
shall be submitted to the Presidency to
forward to the
National Assembly.

68. The financial year of the Agency shall be:
(a) the period starting from the day on which
this Act comes into operation and ending on
the following 31st December;
(b) the period of twelve months commencing
on the first of January and ending on the 31st
December of the subsequent year.

69. The Agency shall cause to be kept all
proper books and records of account of the
income, expenditure, assets and liabilities of
the Agency.

70. The annual accounts of the Agency shall
be prepared, audited and reported upon in
accordance with the Public Audit Act.

71. The Agency shall, at the end of each
financial year cause an annual report to be
prepared.
72. The Agency shall submit the annual report
to the President and the National Assembly
three months after the end of the year to
which it relates.

73. The annual report shall contain, in respect of the year to which it relates:
(a) the financial statements of the Agency;
(b) a description of the activities of the Agency;
(c) such other statistical information as the Agency may consider appropriate relating to the Agency's fund;
(d) any recommendations made by the Agency to MDAs or any person and the action taken;
(e) the impact of the exercise of any of its mandate or function;
(f) any impediments to the achievements of the objects and functions under this Act or any written law; and
(g) Any other information relating to its functions that the Agency considers necessary.

74. The Agency shall cause the annual report to be published and the report shall be publicized in such manner as the Agency may determine.

Part IV – Miscellaneous Provisions

75. Except as provided in this Act, the Agency shall, in the performance of its functions, not

be subject to the direction or control of any person or authority.

76. The Agency shall publish and publicize important information within its mandate affecting the nation. A request for information by a citizen-
(a) shall be addressed to the Director-General or such other person as the Agency may for that purpose designate;
(b) may be subject to the payment of a reasonable fee; and
(c) may be subject to confidentiality requirements of the Agency.

77. Subject to this Act, the Agency may decline to give information to an applicant on the
following grounds -
(a) the request is unreasonable in the circumstances;
(b) the information requested is at a deliberative stage by the Agency;
(c) failure of payment of a prescribed fee; or
(d) failure of the applicant to satisfy confidentiality requirements by the Agency.

78. The right of access to information under the Constitution and any other written law is

limited to the nature and extent specified therein.

79. Every member and employee of the Agency shall sign a confidentiality agreement.

80. The Agency shall, in such manner as it shall consider appropriate, publish a notice for public information specifying:
(a) the location of its principal office; and
(b) its address or addresses, telephone numbers and other means of communication or contact with the Agency.

81. The Agency may request legal advice from the Attorney-General.

82. The Agency may make Regulations for the application of this Act for:
(a) the appointment, including the power to confirm appointments of persons, to any office in respect of which it is responsible under this Act;
(b) the disciplinary control and termination of appointments of employees of the Agency; and
(c) the practice, procedure and code of conduct of the Agency in the exercise of its functions under this Act.

83. All property, assets, rights, liabilities, obligations, agreements and other arrangements existing at the commencement of this Act and vested in, acquired, incurred or entered into by or on behalf of the Special Adviser to the President on Ethics and Values, shall upon the commencement of this Act, be deemed to have vested in or to have been acquired, incurred or entered into by or on behalf of the Agency to the same extent as they were enforceable by or against the Agency before the commencement of the Act.

84. Where the transfer of any property transferred to or vested in the Agency under section 83 is required by any written law to be registered, the Agency shall, within three months from the commencement of this Act or within such other period as the written law may prescribe, apply to the appropriate registering authority for the registration of the transfer and thereupon the registering authority shall, at no cost to the Agency or any person by way of registration fees, stamp or other duties:
(a) make such entries in the appropriate register as shall give effect to the transfer;
(b) where appropriate, issue to the Agency a certificate of title or other statutory evidence of ownership of the property or make such

amendments on such certificates or in the appropriate register as may be necessary; and

(c) make any necessary endorsements on such deeds or other documents as may be presented to such registering authority relating to the title, right or obligation concerned.

12. Conclusion

Although we have coming to the final aspect of this book, I hope that your journey to improve your business ethics is just beginning. Please take a moment to review, develop and update your action plan. This will be a key tool to guide your progress in the days, weeks, months, and years to come. I wish you the best of luck on the rest of your journey in business ethics!

Words of Wisdom
Here are a few thoughts that I would like to leave you with, to accompany you on your journey.
• Juanita Kidd Stout: A person educated in mind and not morals is a menace to society.
• Zig Ziglar: The most important persuasion tool you have in your entire arsenal is integrity.
• James MacGregor Burns: Divorced from ethics, leadership is reduced to management and politics to mere technique.

About the Author

Nicholas has over 18 years proven expertise in development and management of training; especially in sustainable development, general management and construction / health and safety. He has background in a wide range of industries, including construction, agriculture, corporate management, hygiene services and occupational health and safety.

He was instrumental to the coordination of extension workers and service providers training for over 7 years at Farmers Care Project in Swaziland, Southern Africa from 1999, where he remains an ex-officio director to date. He is the Executive Director at the Centre for Regional and International Development and was instrumental to CRID's extended operations in the African sub region and has played key roles in its extension to Asia and the Caribbean.

Nicholas has a MA in Development Studies (work in progress). He also has a B. Agric with specialty in Animal Sciences. He is married and a father of four children. This is his second book in his "The Contemporary Manager Series".

Services

Please be aware that I am happy to help if:

You wish to utilize this information for staff training and development, including:

- Provision of trainer's manual.
- Provision of delegate's handbook.
- Provision of PowerPoint presentation.
- Provision of case study and exercises handouts.
- Provision of training event on the topic or developing your trainers to utilise materials provided.

Your organization wishes to set up a knowledge management unit (KMU), including:

- ✓ Set-up and initial consultations
- ✓ Consultancy work to implement
- ✓ Support towards evaluation and monitoring of KMU
- ✓ Developing your own personalise KM book of knowledge

Any other support you may require utilizing this and other materials corporately.

Business Ethics & its Legal Aspects

For any (or all) of the above, contact me.
Email: nicholas.a@crid.co.uk
Website: www.crid.co.uk

Unit 3, Epsilon House, Laser Quay, Culpeper
Close, Medway City Estate, Kent, ME2 4HU,
United Kingdom.

Useful links

Some helpful reading:

- Business Ethics by Mark C. Vopat & Alan Tomhave

- Business Ethics by K. Praveen Parboteeah and John B. Cullen

- Business Ethics: New Challenges in a Globalised World by Mrs Janet Morrison

- Business Ethics and Corporate Social Responsibility by Paul Griseri and Nina Seppala

- The Value System in Nigeria: Rediscovering the Lost Golden Values by Job Dangana

- The National Assembly, Nigeria – Bill Tracker; https://nass.gov.ng/document/bills

WE PUBLISH BOOKS

Peaches Publications have more than a decade of experience, knowledge and a wealth of information in the book publishing industry. We offer one to one Book Confidence Coaching, to enhance your skill set when formulating your book structure. Let us support your vision in becoming an author and help you to tell your story to friends, family or even the world.

We help budding authors bring their stories to life by providing top quality book services:

Digital publishing	Book publishing
Content	Amazon
Editing	Framework of book
Proof reading	Marketing
Book printing	Research
Sales	Print on demand
Kindle	Book coaching
Copyright Protection	Ghost Writing

www.peachespublications.co.uk

Study Notes

Business Ethics & its Legal Aspects

Study Notes

....

....

....

....

....

....

....

....

....

....

....

....

....

....

Study Notes

Study Notes

....

....

....

....

....

....

....

....

....

....

....

....

....

....

Study Notes

Business Ethics & its Legal Aspects

Study Notes

....
....
....
....
....
....
....
....
....
....
....
....
....
....
....
....
....
....
....
....

103 | P a g e

www.ingramcontent.com/pod-product-compliance
Lightning Source LLC
Chambersburg PA
CBHW070045210526
45170CB00012B/596